The Story of
Bill Mills

The Story of Bill Mills

by
Heather Hurley

Logaston Press

LOGASTON PRESS
Little Logaston Woonton Almeley
Herefordshire HR3 6QH

Published by Logaston Press 2001
in association with
Dayla Liquid Packing Ltd.

ISBN 1 873827 92 X

Set in Times by Logaston Press
and printed in Great Britain by
MFP Design & Print, Manchester

Contents

Acknowledgements

The completion of this history would not have been possible without the help of the Herefordshire Record Office, the Gloucestershire Record Office, Hereford Reference Library, Birmingham City Library Archives, National Paper Museum, the Guildhall Library, Science Museum Library, Whitbread Archives, Herefordshire and Worcestershire Sites and Monuments Records and individual help from Annersley Malley, Peter Bowler, Rosamund Skelton, Ian Standing, Lawrence Hurley, Pat Hughes, Roger and Joan Aston, Joan Snell, the Jenkins family, including the late Brian Jenkins, and staff at Dayla, both past and present.

Introduction

As the 20th century was drawing to a close it became evident that our Mill buildings were going to require some radical thinking to ensure their preservation. The demands on food and drink producing companies made the use of Bill Mills as a factory no longer viable. We needed to find some alternative uses for the buildings which were not only economic but, most importantly, guaranteed their protection and provided the framework for their continuing survival. The commissioning of this book is part of that process, laying down the history in order to set the picture for the present and future.

My family came to Bill Mills in 1958 and soon after purchased the freehold of what was a charming, if not a little run down, cluster of stone, brick and timber buildings. At that time some were derelict, some provided office and residential accommodation but most formed as factory in which beer and soft drinks were bottled, and from which miscellaneous products were sold to the licensed trade. The mill wheel had ceased turning in around 1952, although the signs were everywhere of its belt driving, corn grinding, glorious past.

My father, Brian, dreamed of the days when he would be able to make use of all the property and to make the wheel turn again and, in between time spent making a living, he planned the renovation of his little community. In due course the stables, coach house and paper drying lofts were converted to holiday cottages, creating a small business and resurrecting some picturesque buildings. By the 1980s he had also rebuilt the wheel and had it frequently running, re-kindling the sounds of its hard working past. Brian retired from the drinks business in 1986 and then spent much of his time researching Bill Mills and it is his work that became the seed corn for this book.

At the time of publishing, the future direction of the Mill at Bill Mills is still not absolutely certain. We have proposed various avenues including a working paper museum which unfortunately failed due to the enormous cost of renovating what have become totally empty buildings. We have investigated the possibilities of hotels, training centres and offices, to no avail. It is now most likely that Bill Mills will be sympathetically renovated as a group of residential dwellings. The wheel area, along with its workings, is guaranteed to be kept alive and made available for viewing when the current work is complete.

And so Bill Mills enters into a new chapter as an attractive and historic feature in beautiful surroundings. The future seems secure and we hope that if you enjoy this book you will take the time to visit The Mill at Bill Mills.

Ian Jenkins
October 2001

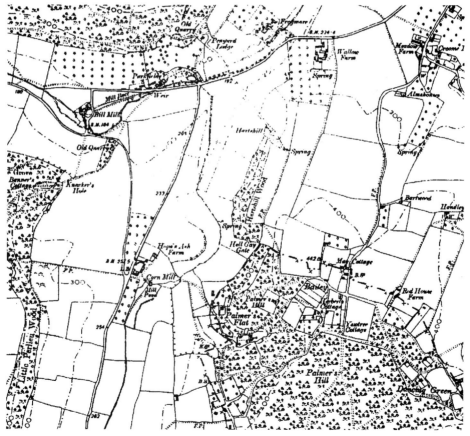

Bill Mills as depicted on the 1887 Ordnance Survey map

Chapter I

The Castle Brook Valley

Once more following the road, we come to a cross-road, and instead of
turning to the left, which would take us directly to Ross, we go on past
Coughton into a deep and narrow valley, bounded on each side by
wooded hills, and winding through them in a most graceful curve.

George Strong, 1863

In a rural corner of Herefordshire three miles from the market town of Ross-
on-Wye stands a picturesque cluster of buildings called Bill Mills. They lie in
the parish of Weston-under-Penyard, near its boundary with Hope Mansell,
amidst delightful scenery. For centuries the site has been occupied by a mill
which has been powered by the swift clear waters of the Castle Brook, a
stream which flows through a deep and attractive valley between the wooded
hills of Chase, Penyard, Howle and the Lea Bailey which form part of the
Forest of Dean.

It has been suggested that the Castle Brook valley formed an ancient
meander of the River Wye, but due to climatic change many thousands of years
ago it was cut off. The geology of the district is mainly Old Red Sandstone
which produces a rich soil, ideal for all types of farming. Its distinctive reddish
colour is a familiar characteristic of the Herefordshire landscape, noticeable in
ploughed fields and recognised in stone-built walls and buildings. Hidden
amongst the trees on the wooded slopes of the Castle Brook valley are rocky
outcrops of conglomerate, known locally as Plumb Pudding Stone.

The surrounding hills all rise to over 600 feet and provide a scenic topographical feature where man has left his mark since prehistoric days: an Iron

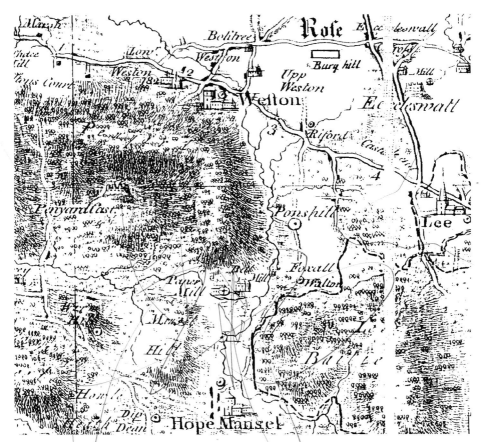

Taylor's map of 1786 showing the paper mill at Bill Mills, the house now called Parkfields, Castle Brook and Penyard Castle

Age hillfort on Chase Hill, an ancient earthwork on Howle Hill, the remains of a medieval castle on Penyard Hill. It was this castle that undoubtedly provided the name of the brook which, over the years, powered several mills along its course. Apart from the mill at Bill Mills, there was a corn mill at Hope Mansell which was demolished in the 1950s, 'three water corn mills lying under one roof' at Coughton, which became dis-used by 1904, and a tuck mill called Inage at Cobray. In Walford the present saw mills stand on the the site of a former corn mill in use until around 1946.

Whilst the area around the valley now appears predominately rural, in the past it has seen has much industrial activity. To the north-east of Penyard Hill is the Roman iron-making site of *Ariconium*, and in a recess above Bill Mills on the slopes of Penyard Hill, a Roman coin was found in 1793 lying in the cinders of an ancient bloomery. Recently, iron slag at Bill Mills has been identified as dating from the bloomery period, which spans from Roman Times to around 1600. (Bloomery describes small scale furnaces which smelt iron ore without melting it.) Slightly further afield, iron ore mines existed at Wigpool and old lime kilns at Hope Mansell.

From archaeological finds and records it is evident that a Roman road existed near Bill Mills, leading from *Ariconium* across the Wigg Meadows to Frogmore, where iron slag surfacing has been identified. This route probably continued past Street Farm in Hope Mansell to the iron ore mines at Wigpool. It is considered that another route from Frogmore followed the Castle Brook valley past Bill Mills and Coleraine Farm before crossing the River Wye at Walford—the 'Welsh-ford'—to Goodrich.

The present road through the Castle Brook valley leads from Ryeford lying on the Gloucester road, which formerly served as the main thoroughfare from London to South Wales and Hereford. From Ryeford the valley road passes Parkfields and

Forging iron at a bloomsmithy in Germany, c.1550. The workers in the centre left of the illustration are using wooden mallets to beat bloom taken from a furnace (top) to reduce it to smaller pieces which are then reheated in a forge (lower right) and shaped into bars

makes an exaggerated bend around Bill Mills to a minor crossways, where an abandoned route led from Ross to the Forest of Dean. Until recently this was marked with an upright stone, possibly the remains of an ancient cross or mark stone. In a survey of Dean Forest made in 1281 this stone was recorded as the Cross of Koctere marking the highway to Alton in Ross. From here the road proceeds past Cobrey and through Coughton to Walford.

Another early route has been discovered, leading from Bill Mills to the church at Weston-under-Penyard, which by 1840 was known as Ugdon Lane. The route is preserved as a public footpath and may be followed through the fields, where traces of the lane may be identified. Earlier references to the name include 'Hogge of Bilmill in Hogdon' in 1549 and 'Common Hugdons' in 1699.

Two developments were proposed in the 19th century which, if carried out, would have transformed the Castle Brook valley. In 1822 and 1824 'New Lines of Road' were planned leading from Old Forge to The Lea. If adopted this would have influenced the future network of roads and eliminated the acute bend at Bill Mills. The other development was proposed during the formation of the Hereford, Ross, Gloucester Railway in the 1850s, to construct a line from The Lea, along the Castle Brook valley, through Walford to Ross. This route was subsequently abandoned in favour of a line through Weston-under-Penyard.

Upright stone at Castle Brook
(Alfred Watkins)

Chapter II

The Development of Bill Mills

The Miller was a,chap of sixteen stone,
A great stout fellow big in brawn and bone.
He did, well out of them, for he could go
And win the ram at any wrestling show.
Geoffrey Chaucer, 1484

Whilst the name 'Weston-under-Penyard' describes the position of the village as west of *Ariconium* and below Penyard Hill and Pontshill is probably named after Pant's Hill, the derivation of Bill Mills is difficult to understand. A rector of Weston-under-Penyard in 1927 who discovered the remains of a Roman road near Bill Mills suggested that the name may have originated from *Villa Milliaries*—the 'Villa at the Mill Stone'. Another possibility is that the name of the mill may have evolved from the Old English *billere* an early name of several water plants including watercress, or from 'bylte' meaning 'a heap, a small hill'. Such a derivation is found in other names such as Billfordes Close and Bille Meadow at Lea, and Bilbrook in Somerset.

Weston-under-Penyard and Pontshill were recorded in the *Domesday Book* as held by Durand, the first Norman sheriff of Gloucestershire, but no mill was mentioned. In 1228 the earliest preambulations of the Forest of Dean were made to delineate the forest boundaries where forest laws applied which recorded that the forest extended north-east to Newent and north to Ross including the parish of Weston-under-Penyard. From other sources it has been ascertained that forges existed at Hope Mansell along with numerous iron forges and mills in the Forest of Dean including one near Guns Mills.

The first known specific mention of Bill Mills appears in a Hope Mansell document dated 1362 which records 'a highway leading to Bulimulle'. In 1367, during the reign of Edward III, Nicholas le Castell granted 'all his lands and tenements in Poushill, Bullmyll, and Hope Maloisell' to Geoffrey de Caple, the Rector of Mitcheldean. These early references suggest an established mill at Bill Mills powered by water either for grinding corn, the manufacturing of iron, or for both uses.

Watermills were established on streams and rivers where a consistent water flow could be guaranteed, with the supply of water contained by damming. Artificial water courses were constructed, which diverted the water from the main flow along a leat that led to the mill to power the waterwheel. From here the water returned to the stream via the tail race. The Castle Brook was ideal for such a development.

Early documentation of Bill Mills does not describe its type, but recent evidence suggests that Bill Mills originated as a medieval ironmill. After the Black Death of 1348 there was a shortage of labour which provided an impetus for the construction of water-powered mills. In the Colchester Papers (at Gloucester Record Office) a Walter Castell is recorded as an ironmonger in 1368 followed by the John Thomas family of 'Bylmyll' in the 15th century when Roger Berrowe was the 'smith'. Mills were often converted from one type to another—Guns Mills at Abenhall in Gloucestershire had many uses throughout its long history.

By 1418 Richard Walwyn, who had acquired Hellens at Much Marcle a few years earlier, held 'all rights in a mill called Bullemulle in Weston'. His father, Thomas Walwyn, claimed to have owned land 'stretching towards the

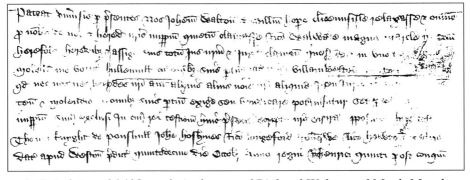

A Quitclaim of 1418 made in favour of Richard Walwyn of Much Marcle for all rights in a mill called Bullemill

Settlement by agreement of 1572 between Sir Richard Walwyn and Thomas Walwyn, his youngest son

cathedrals of Gloucester and Hereford', although when he died two-thirds of the estate apparently reverted to the crown. However, the family remained a major landowner and their estate at Weston-under-Penyard, called 'Byll Myll', passed through the family to another Richard whose wife Alice is probably the lady who held the Abenhall mills between 1471 and 1518. Eventually by 1566 'Bylmyll' was inherited by Sir Richard Walwyn, knighted by Queen Mary during the 1550s.

Sir Richard's second marriage caused family conflict and an expensive law suit which led to his eldest son being disinherited and Sir Richard made a Settlement by Agreement dated 1572, leaving his properties — including 'Byll Myll' — to his youngest son, Thomas. After the father's death in 1578 the eldest son managed to claim his inheritance, and in turn the estate passed to his son, Ely. Unfortunately Ely was unable to pay his father's debts so his properties in Ledbury, Ashperton and Weston-under-Penyard ware sold to various creditors in 1594. It appears that the mill and other properties in the manor of Weston-under-Penyard were acquired by Gilbert Talbot, 7th Earl of Shrewsbury. These powerful Talbots of Goodrich, Eccleswall and Penyard castles had been prominent in the defence of the Welsh borders and had been created earls of Shrewsbury in the 15th century. At the time of this transfer of family ownership, it appears that Thomas Lloyd and his family occupied Bill Mill.

In 1603 an outrage was committed in Ross by 'some of the workmen in yor hnors. iron works at your ffurnace of Billmelene', confirming an iron-working site at Bill Mills. A few years later, in 1616, Gilbert Talbot died and his properties were inherited by his daughters. Elizabeth, his second daughter, conveyed the Herefordshire estates including Bill Mills to her husband, Henry de Grey, Earl of Kent.

Before 1638 'one messuage, 66 acres of land, 15 acres of meadow, 18 acres of pasture and 12 acres of wood in Weston under Penyard and Bill Myll' were in the tenure of John Keyse, William Meek and Walter Lloyde. These premises, together with land in the tenure of Christopher Westerdale and Thomas Bonnor, were 'held of Henry Earl of Kent and Elizabeth Countess of Kent, his wife, as of their manor of Weston under Penyard', and were 'so seised' by James Hawkins from Lydbrook.

During the Civil War the mill, like others in the neighbourhood, may have been firstly damaged in raids of 1646 and then put out of business in 1650. In 1646, at Drybrook, acts of cruelty from foraging parties were recorded, including the striking out of one person's eyes when the person concerned refused to hand over a flitch of bacon. In 1650, with the government trying to retain timber for ship-building, the committe of the House of Commons charged with the care of the Forest of Dean, tried to suppress and demolish all the iron forges in the Forest. The value of the 'losses and damage sustained by the inhabitants' of Weston-under-Penyard eventually amounted to £742 5s. 8d. during the course of the Civil War. After this upheaval, when property changed hands the Westerdales from Taynton in Gloucestershire were at 'Billmill' with the Lloyds working the mill. Although it is understood that the Lloyds 'migrated to Abenhall' at a later date, it appears they may have moved earlier as a Mrs. Lloyd leased 'mills and fforges and meadow' at Flaxley in 1693. However, many Lloyds were recorded in Weston at the 'Meadow' and the 'Wallo' long after this date.

Chapter III

The Paper Makers

Rags make paper,
Paper makes money,
Money makes banks,
Banks make loans,
Loans make beggars,
Beggars make rags.

Anon

Recent evidence and research suggests that paper makers in the Welsh Borders and the West Midlands were established earlier than the early 18th century as previously considered. When Caxton sat up his printing works in London during the 15th century he obtained his paper from the Continent, although a few of his successors did use home produced paper. With an expansion in economic and industrial activity, improved communications, and a growth in trade from around 1500, an increased amount of paper was required for letters, documents and records. This led to a demand for paper making which spread across Britain.

Papermills were located beside running water, needed for power and as a raw material. The quantity of water was not enough by itself, it was the quality of 'quick and clear streams' that was important and where this was available the papermaking industry thrived and developed. In Tudor and Stuart times papermills were often converted from mills previously used for other purposes. Before 1642 a paper mill was converted from a furnace at Perry Barr in the West Midlands. It was not uncommon to find two types of

*Indenture of 30 August 1698 between John Viney and Daniel Seymour
for the sale of the mill*

mills working under one roof, especially if papermaking was on a small scale, and this may have been the early arrangement at Bill Mills, where paper-making is recorded from 1682.

Towards the end of the 17th century Henry Westerdale held the Bill Mills estate. In 1661 his daughter, Mary, married John Viney, a gentleman from Gloucester, born in 1653, who was educated at Oxford and called to the bar in 1677. It seems probable that John Viney acquired Bill Mills either through a Marriage Settlement or after Henry Westerdale died in 1682. At this time Thomas Faux was the tenant of the mill and possibly the first papermaker, who continued there until his death in 1696 at the age of 80. He was followed by Joseph Smith 'Papermaker' in 1698 when John Viney, after the death of his wife, sold Bill Mills and purchased Little Taynton and Willington Court in Gloucestershire.

The largest portion of the Bill Mills estate was purchased by Thomas Bonnor, whose family, already well established in Weston-under-Penyard, became more prominent at a later date. The mill, described as 'a messuage dwelling house or tenement and paper mill with the appurtenances commonly called Bill Mill alias Billmills with two gardens', was sold separately for £168

Inventory of Thomas Faux, papermaker, 1696

to Daniel Seymour of the Bollin, Walford. He immediately resold the property for the same amount to Richard Bond of Cobrey, a neighbouring estate in the same parish.

Richard Bond was from a landowning family originally from Newland in Gloucestershire, who had acquired the Cobrey estate around 1670. On his land were other mills including 'water corn Mills lying under one roof', so it was in his interest to purchase the papermill with rights to regulate 'the stream of water and watercourses running to drive the said mill and the ponds pounds stanks and banks thereto belonging and free liberty to cast up the dyrt under and soyle upon the said banks for the cleansing and the clearing of the brook there from time to time when need shall require so far as the lands of one Thomas Bonnor'. Under the ownership of Richard Bond, Bill Mill operated as a papermill run by Joseph Smith at a yearly rent of £13 10s.

The existing mill site on the Castle Brook proved to be extremely suitable for papermaking. There was a constant supply of water for power, plenty of clean water for papermaking, a good flow of air through the valley for the drying process, and presumably a source of rags (then used for papermaking)

Early papermaking, circa *17th century*

The opening paragraphs of the abstract of title 'to a certain Paper Mill called Bill Mill' prepared in 1831 for Joseph Lloyd, which commences with details of the sale by John Viney in 1698

available from the surrounding villages and towns. Communications by road and river were adequate with access to the Forest of Dean, the market towns of Ross and Monmouth, and the cities of Hereford and Gloucester.

Early papermaking by hand was a skilled and complicated process. The cotton and linen rags were sorted, soaked in water, placed in heaps and allowed to rot. After thorough washing they were pulped in the stamping mill powered by water. The pulped fibres ware conveyed from storage tanks to a large vat where they were formed into sheets with the aid of a mould. These were then taken to drain, before being placed in a wooden screw press. When the surplus water had been removed the sheets were taken to the drying lofts, where shutters could be adjusted to control the air flow. Further treatment including sizing followed before the sheets of finished paper were taken to the storeroom.

Rag cutting in the 18th century

It is possible to create an approximate picture of Bill Mills at the start of the 18th century by using the information gleaned from documents, existing architectural features and details from other papermills of this period. In 1714 the property consisted of a dwelling house and papermill with two gardens

An early papermaking machine

A drawing indicating various stages of the papermaking process

occupied by Joseph Smith and his wife Mary. With their son and two daughters they probably lived in the existing black and white timber-framed building which dates from 1700. Apart from the stone-built basement there is no evidence of another floor, or of any chimneys, but the building has been drastically altered and incorporated into a much later structure.

The 18th-century site was much smaller than it is today, and buildings would have housed a rag store, drying loft, a press and vat room with the mill displaying an exterior waterwheel. In 1727 a 'Great Sluice Dam' was erected to keep the water 'at an equal height and level' in the millpond, and a stream of water was made to 'run in a straight line' from the 'Bridge on the Millpond of the said Richard Bond belonging to his paper mill' at Bill Mills. This ran through the lands of Thomas Bonnor who agreed not to interfere with the flow of water or cut down any growth on its banks. These arrangements were necessary in order to keep the water clean for papermaking, and to regulate a supply of water for Bond's other mills in Walford. (These alterations may

Drying paper

have changed the ground level around the mill and redirected the line of the water courses.)

In 1714 at the end of Queen Anne's reign Richard Bond's estate comprised of 'Four Messuages Four Cottages 5 Gardens 3 Watercornmills 2 Papermills 5 Gardens 6 Orchards 200 Acres of Land 70 Acres of Meadow 20 Acres of Pasture 12 Acres of Wood and Common of Pasture for all Cattle within the Parishes of Walford Ross Weston under Penyard and Hopemansell'. Bond served as High Sheriff for Herefordshire, and after his death in the 1730s, Elizabeth, his sole heir, inherited his properties and subsequently married Gabriel Hanger in 1737.

Gabriel was the son of Sir George Hanger of Driffield in Gloucestershire and before his marriage he served in the East India Company. When he returned to England he became a Whig MP. His wealthy cousin, the Baroness of Coleraine, died in 1754 and left him her property but not the peerage which had become extinct. At a later date he applied for the Irish baronetcy of Coleraine, his cousin's old title, and was created a Baron of the second creation. Through marriage Gabriel had acquired the Cobrey estate which included one papermill known as 'Bill Mills Mill with two Gardens' and 'Furnaces, new mills, cole mine and mill' in Walford.

16

Chapter IV

One Hundred Years of Papermaking

Leaving the main road the second turning on the left, after passing the 12 mile-stone, cross Ponsill's Marsh, by Billmill Lodge and paper mill, through the village of Walford. In this route, Penyard park and chase are on the right, and Bishop's Wood on the left. The whole ride is diversified by rich and ever varying objects; and in summer time, the traveller is refreshed by the protection he may derive from the grateful shades, which for a considerable part of the way defend him from the beams of the sun; whilst on either side he will find ample scope for contemplation.

Bonnor, 1798

Joseph Smith, the papermaker, was replaced around 1730 by Thomas Parker at a yearly rent still of £13 10s. Parker was the son of Thomas and Mary of Weston-under-Penyard, he married a girl called Ann and in 1731 took on an apprentice named William Morris. Three children were born to the couple including Thomas in 1734, who eventually followed his father at the papermill during the mid-18th century. Another relative recorded at Bill Mills was 'Thomas Parker the Younger' who married Sarah Thompson from Ruardean.

During the 18th century there was a great expansion in papermaking due to a rising population and an increase in trade and industry. Greater quantities were required for bills, ledgers, account books, letters and for the book trade printing technical, scientific and literary works. An example of paper used at the Blue Coat Charity School is shown in the account of 1768. Newspapers increased in size and variety for a growing volume of readers, and more

An account showing, below the sub-total of £14 10 shillings, the types of paper used in 1768 at the Blue Coat Charity School in Ross

coarse paper was required for the wrapping of goods in shops and other commercial enterprises. At the other end of the range, better quality paper was required and so mills were improved.

Other local papermills operating at this time included one at Tressack near Hoarwithy in Herefordshire, Guns Mills at Abenhall in Gloucestershire, Ruthlin Mill at Rockfield in Monmouthshire, Rodmore Mill in the Forest of Dean and a handfull of mills in the lower Wye Valley. Further afield paper was being produced at Mortimers Cross on the River Lugg, Hurcutt Mill on the Wannerton Brook, Hay Mills on the River Teme and at the Ludford Paper Mill also on the Teme. There is sufficient information to suggest paper mills at Marstow on the Luke Brook, at Cusop on the Dulas Brook and at Walford on the Castle Brook.

The owner of Bill Mills, Lord Gabriel Coleraine, died in 1773, and by his will entailed his estates on his daughter and three sons, who were described

Details of the auction sale of Cowberry, Coaton Mill and Bill Mill in the Hereford Journal *for 10 March 1774*

by Walpole as 'unnatural wretches'. The eldest son— 'a dissolute fellow'— became Lord John Coleraine and managed to legally break the entailment to pay debts amounting to £26,000. This was settled with the proceeds of the sale of 'Cowberry', 'Coaton Mill' and 'Bill Mill now let to Thomas Parker at £301. per ann. in exceeding good repair, and constantly supplied with water', as well as 'Wruxton' and other properties in Newland and Hope Mansell.

After losing her husband and property Lady Elizabeth Coleraine was recorded as living at Windsor Castle where she died in 1780. Bill Mills was purchased by 'Thomas Parker, paper-maker and Elizabeth his wife' for £350 in 1775, and Cobrey was sold to Charles Trusted, also the existing tenant. The papermill appears to have been extended to include 'Drying Houses and Stables' sometime before Thomas died in 1779 leaving his son, Richard, to run the business.

In 1786 the 'Paper Mill' is depicted with an external waterwheel on Taylor's map, and the existing overshot wheel is understood to date from this period. It was constructed of iron and oak and measured 15 ft by 5 ft, though has since been modified and restored. A Sun Fire Insurance Policy dated 1782 describes the papermill buildings as follows:

dwelling house Workhouse and Ragloft adjoining each other
Brewhouse separate
Paper Mill separate
The above brick Stoned and tiled
Two Drying houses adjoining each other separate
tiled and thatched

The buildings, household goods, utensils and stock were insured for a total of £600, this being nearly half the amount paid by Joseph Lloyd at Guns Mills in 1780.

Richard Parker, the new young papermaker, was born in 1759, and after the death of his father inherited the papermill at a time when traditional paper-making had reached its peak of production. In 1782 Richard married Jane Smith from the Hill at Weston-under-Penyard, and their first child was born a year later. After the early death of his wife in 1786, he married her sister, Susannah, but shortly after the birth of their fourth child named Thomas, both mother and son died. Richard continued at Bill Mills and in 1797 took out a loan of £400 'upon security of the premises'.

The increased use of paper eventually led to a shortage in the supply of rags, so huge quantities were imported from America, Eastern Europe and Russia. The unpleasant and dirty work of sorting and grading them was mainly carried out by women, who were in constant danger of contacting infectious diseases. Other raw materials made from plants and vegetables were tried, and old ropes, fishing nets and sail cloth derived from hemp were often also used. Unfortunately it has not been possible to establish which materials were used at Bill Mills, but the use of rags appears to be the most likely.

With Richard Parker at 'Bill Mills Mill' in the 1790s, the adjoining 'Bill Mill Lodge', now called Parkfields, was still occupied by the Bonnor family. They were closely related to Thomas Bonnor a topographical engraver who became 'one of the ablest topographical artists of his time'. His work flourished between 1763 and 1807 with his fine plates appearing in books on Worcester, Somerset, Gloucester and Devon. He also wrote and illustrated the 'Perspective Views' of Goodrich Castle published in 1798, which features

The signatures of Richard Parker and Joseph Lloyd, papermakers in 1808

44/7189 Richard Parker of Weston under Penyard in the

16/- County of Hereford Paper maker, on his now dwelling house

Michas 1782 Workhouse & Rag loft adjoining each other situated aforesaid

18/- not exceeding One hundred & thirty pounds — 130

How Household Goods therein only not exceeding One hundred pounds — 100

Utensils & Stock therein only not exceeding One hundred & forty pounds 140

Brewhouse Seperate not exceeding Twenty pounds — 20

Utensils & Stock therein only not exceeding Ten pounds — 10

Paper Mill seperate not exceeding Fifty pounds — 50

Utensils & Stock therein only not exceeding Fifty pounds — 50

The above Brick stone & tiled Two Drying houses adjoining each

other seperate tiled & thatched not exceeding Fifty pounds — 50

Utensils & Stock therein only not exceeding Fifty pounds — 50

J. Pearse C. Burrukr H. Watts   £ 600

Details of Richard Parker's valuation for insurance purposes in 1782,
producing a total of £600

many local scenes. His neighbour, Richard Parker, subscribed to this informative and attractive publication.

During Richard Parker's last few years at Bill Mills, he was often visited by Charles Heath, the Monmouth bookseller and antiquarian. In a 'flower-woven' garden they 'sate down to smoke a pipe together' and obviously enjoyed one anothers company. At the beginning of the 19th century Heath described Bill Mills:

> In a cozy spot ..., embosomed between Penyard and other lofty woods in this parish, hid from day's garish eye, is a Paper manufactory, which, when I came to Monmouth, and for many years after, was the property and residence of my much valued friend, Mr. Richard Parker, distinguished among the first *papietiers* in the surrounding district, and under whose roof, from his hospitality, Weston is rendered more dear to my recollection, as well as by his introduction to families before unknown to me.

Although Parker lived to the grand old age of 93, he retired from the paper-mill in 1808 when only 49 and sold the premises for £1,600 to Joseph Lloyd, the established papermaker from Guns Mills.

Thomas Lloyd, father of Joseph, was a descendant of the family who had occupied Bill Mills during the 17th century. Since settling in Abenhall the Lloyds had extended their business, and were making paper at Postlip, Sudely and Awre in Gloucestershire. Joseph, their eldest son, was born at Abenhall in 1741, and married Mary Robinson from Littledean in 1771. Described as 'an amiable lady with a genteel fortune' she made a suitable wife for Joseph who was improving his social position and who duly went into partnership with his father. Their second daughter, Mary, lived to the age of 99 years. She married Captain George Adams, who was instrumental in establishing the British and Foreign School at Ross in 1837.

With the Lloyds' experience of papermaking on a larger scale, it seems probable that alterations were made at Bill Mills from 1808. New methods were then being introduced into papermaking including the use of beater engines to pulp the rags quicker and more efficiently, and the use of varied chemicals for bleaching purposes. This may be the date that the waterwheel was enclosed and the 'engine, presses and all working materials' were installed. A detailed plan of c.1820 confirms the extent of the buildings, and the enclosure of the waterwheel. The surviving 'filter tiles' must also date from this period.

By the end of the 18th century Hurcott Mill in Worcestershire boasted the use of 2 engines, 2 vats, 4 iron presses, a wood screw, spacious drying rooms, and a rag house four storeys high, and a later inventory suggests that the waterwheel had became enclosed. In 1803 Joseph Lloyd's mills in Gloucestershire already had engine and bleaching houses plus finishing rooms, sorting lofts, sizing houses, warehouses, offices and many outbuildings. At this date Lloyd recorded his reams of white and coloured paper, and his stock of fine rags, coloured rags, sacking, shavings, old papers and ropes in the 'Sorting Loft'.

Joseph lloyd's watermark dated 1816 from Ross Poor Rate records

It seems appropriate here to mention the Excise Duty paid on paper. It was unpopular as seen as a taxation on knowledge, affecting books, newspapers and other printed sources required for learning. Although reforms ware made during the 18th century, the duty was increased during the Napoleonic Wars. In 1816 an Excise List of papermakers records the Herefordshire Collection with their Excise Number including: Bill Mills - 146, Tressach - 147, Mortimers Cross - 148, Hall Mill at Awre - 142, Guns Mills - 143 and Walford Mill in Leintwardine - 152. Watermarks recently discovered in Ross documents only show Lloyd's name and dates of 1809, 1816, 1818 and 1823 on paper that was almost certainly produced at Bill Mills.

In 1821 William Cobbett of *Rural Rides* fame noted:

> Down the deep and beautiful valley between Penyard Hill and the hills on the side of the Forest of Dean, there runs a stream of water. On that stream of water there is a paper-mill. In that paper-mill there is a set of workmen. That set of workmen do, I am told, take the *Register*, and have taken it for years! It was to these good and sensible men, it is supposed, that the ringing of the bells of Weston church, upon my arrival, was to be ascribed; for nobody that I visited had any knowledge of the cause. What a subject for lamentation with corrupt hypocrites! That even on this secluded spot there should be a leaven of common sense!

Cobbett edited the *Political Register*, an independent radical journal obviously read by Lloyd's employees at Bill Mills.

Before purchasing Bill Mills in 1806 Joseph Lloyd, Senior, had already moved to Mount Craig in the Herefordshire parish of Goodrich. When he died in 1828 at the age of 89 he was known as 'Joseph Lloyd of Abenhall and Mount Craig' and was buried at Abenhall. His son Thomas who served as a Justice of the Peace continued to live at Mount Craig, and another son, Joseph Junior, made arrangements to sell Bill Mills to Thomas Bright, a corn miller from Coughton in Walford.

The 'Arrangements' dated August 1831 made between Lloyd and Bright concerned the sale of 'All that Dwelling House Mill Outbuildings and premises called Bill Mill' for a sum of £1,300 to be paid 'before the second day of February next'. Lloyd agreed 'to remove and take away the Engine, Presses and all working materials in and about the Mill or which have been used in working the same save and except the Vat, Furnaces, pipes Machinery and Chests'.

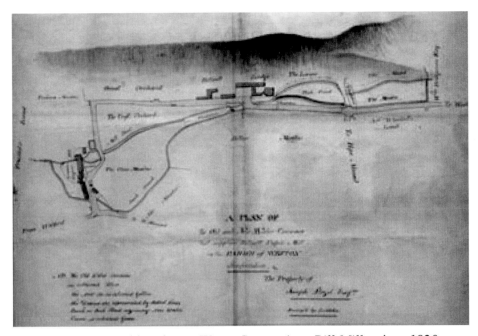

Plan of 'The Old and New Water Courses', at Bill Mills, circa *1820s*

This marked the end of Bill Mills as a papermill, at a time when many small mills went out of existence. In Herefordshire Tressach Mill in Hentland was advertised as a 'Bone Crushing Mill', and Walford Mill in Leintwardine was listed as a cornmill in 1851. The papermill at Mortimer's Cross had already ceased producing paper by 1824, but Gunns Mills in the Forest of Dean continued to produce paper until the end of the 19th century after being modernised and converted to steam. This collapse in numbers of small paper-mills was partly due to competition from bigger and better sited mills which incorporated new machinery that could produce larger quantities of cheap paper, but was also due to a lack of rags. Although in Herefordshire bales of rags were still being transported by barges along the River Wye in 1827, in 1832 rag merchants in London, Manchester and Birmingham went bankrupt including James Pegg who had only been discharged from a Debtor's Prison in 1829.

Chapter V

Corn Milling

Here is the mill with the humming of thunder,
Here is the weir with the wonder of foam,
Here is the sluice with the race running under—
Marvellous places, though handy to home!
R.L. Stevenson, 1885

In 1832 Thomas Bright the miller from Coughton Mill in Walford purchased 'all that Messuage Dwelling House or Tenement and Paper Mill with the apportionment commonly called Bill Mills alias Bill Mill Mills' by raising a mortgage of £1,000 from the former owner, Joseph Lloyd. While Bright was converting the old papermill, the cornmill at Coughton was occupied by a farmer by the name of William Howell. It was later run by James Hope for Henry Thomas Bussell, a corn, cake, seed, flour merchant, miller and wool dealer in Ross.

By 1838 Bright had the additional use of a piece of arable land in Hope Mansell, but the site was almost entirely surrounded by land belonging to Thomas Trusted of Parkfield House. It appears that various alterations were made by Bright to the mill buildings and watercourses to make the mill suitable for corn milling, and the domestic accommodation was moved to the south of the mill as shown on the 1838 Tithe Map. Three years later Thomas Bright was recorded in the census as a mealman of 50 years of age living at Bill Mills with his wife, Mary, and their five daughters aged between 12 and 20.

In the 1851 census Thomas was recorded as a farmer of 130 acres residing at 'Bill Mill House' with his wife and four daughters with one house servant and employing four labourers. The miller, William Nichols, was living at Bill Mill Cottage. During the 1850s Thomas also acquired Croft Meadow, Hollow Meadow and Lower Field, but by 1857 he had retired to Little Sandyway in Weston-under-Penyard. Having established Bill Mills as a 'Corn Grist Mill' he sold the premises for £1,600 to Thomas Wintle, an up and coming corn merchant from Mitcheldean in Gloucestershire. Thomas Bright remained at Sandyway, and after the death of his 'dear wife Mary' he was looked after by his housekeeper Eliza Jennings and a servant Emma Baker. When he died in 1864 his daughters benefited from his will, but Eliza was left £200 and Emma £20, and 'a proper suit of mourning each if respectively living with me at my decease'.

At the time that Bright sold the mill in 1857 the present overshot water-wheel measuring 15 by 5 feet was the only source of power—grinding the corn, hoisting the sacks and bagging the flour. A subsequent owner of the mill, Brian Jenkins, explained the working of this watermill:

> A sack of corn would be received and lifted to the bin floor by means of the sack hoist; this hoist being driven by belt and pulley off the crown wheel. The grain is tipped into a bin and gravity feeds into the hopper; the damsel is driven by the stone nut and spins against the shoe causing the latter to vibrate which in turn causes the grain to drop evenly into the eye (centre) of the stones rather than drop in lumps.
>
> The bed stone is fixed whilst the running stone turns and the faces of both stones are 'dressed' i.e. furrows are cut into the stones at an angle against each other and the set of stones is completely enclosed in a wooden 'tun'. When the grain drops into the eye, the action of the stones forces the grain through the furrows, first crushing and then grinding, to the outside of the stones where the resultant flour drops down a chute to the bagging floor. In the case of the mill at Bill Mill, some or all of the flour is conveyed by the worm conveyor (auger) and vertical conveyor back to the floor(s) above for further treatment, perhaps for white flour or for grading. After treatment, the meal is again conveyed and drops back to the bagging floor.
>
> The tentering is a device to enable the miller to adjust the quality of his flour; the arrangement allows the distance between the stones to be adjusted thus allowing for a coarse or fine meal.
>
> There is a further simple arrangement whereby the vibration of the shoe could be adjusted to the miller's liking.
>
> The dressing of the stones was most important and often carried out by travelling craftsmen. It entailed lifting the stones and hand cutting

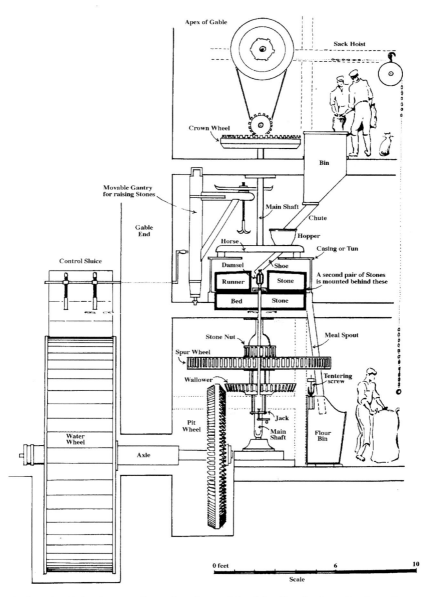

Apex of Gable

Sack Hoist

Crown Wheel

Bin

Movable Gantry
for raising Stones

Main Shaft

Chute

Gable
End

Horse

Hopper

Casing or Tun

Control Sluice

Damsel

Shoe

A second pair of Stones
is mounted behind these

Runner   Stone

Bed   Stone

Stone Nut

Meal Spout

Spur Wheel

Tentering
screw

Wallower

Pit
Wheel

Jack

Water
Wheel

Main
Shaft

Flour
Bin

Axle

| 0 feet | | 6 | 10 |

Scale

*A sketch of the internal mechanism of Le Moulin de Quetivel on Jersey,
used by Brian Jenkins as an example of corn milling similar to the workings
of Bill Mills*

27

the furrows with an iron tool 'stone bill'. The bill would need frequent sharpening and the workman would be [positioned] adjoining a sharpening stone (driven by belts etc).

Contemporary descriptions of corn milling during the late 19th century have been difficult to find, but recollections although tinged with romanticism provide some insight. One writer recalls the unique sound of 'the curious creaking of a waterwheel added to the boom of the water racing over the pondhead', and 'the creak, creak, creak of the wheel and the roar of the water as it wrenches and worries over the paddles'. Inside the miller hoisted sacks of corn to the top floor, where the grain was stored and then fed through a chute to be ground by the millstones. From time to time, the miller tested the grade and felt 'between his forefinger and thumb, the meal as it fell into the sack'.

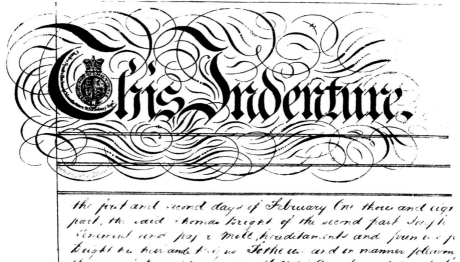

The opening part of a conveyance of August 1857
between Thomas Bright and Thomas Wintle

In most mills 'the millwright was responsible for the upkeep and proper working of the mill. He was a skilled craftsman in both wood and metal; and although most practised millers dressed their own stones, dressing the grind-stones of the mill to keep them in a condition to grind the corn effectively was often done by the millwright.' It was important that the stones did not run dry as explained by a Victorian miller: 'the stones have to be fed with corn all the time. If the runner stone revolves on the bed stone with nothing in between to grind there's soon trouble because the stones get hot and sparks fly out; and there is no lack in a mill of something to catch fire very quickly'.

In the 1860s traditional milling by waterpower was still flourishing in the Wye valley and the Forest of Dean. Coughton Mill and Walford Flour Mill also lay on the Castle Brook, whilst there was the Old Mill at Goodrich on the Garron, and the Rudhall Mill, Foxall Mill and the One Mill at Ross on the Rudhall Brook were still waterpowered. However, the Ross Town Mills in Brookend had been re-erected by 1865 and a '12-horse-power Steam Engine' installed.

After Thomas Wintle purchased Bill Mills as a corn mill in 1857 he conveyed the business to his brother, Alfred, in 1862. In his early twenties Alfred traded as a 'Corndealer, Maltster and Miller', living at Bill Mill House with a housekeeper and servant. His miller, George Abell, lived with his wife and family in Bill Mill Cottage. These details show that malting had commenced at Bill Mills since the Wintles purchased the premises, which may have prompted Alfred's brother, Thomas, to start the Forest Brewery at Mitcheldean in 1868.

The Forest Brewery was established on a site found to be 'exceptionally favourable' with the advantage of a supply of 'excellent water' obtained from the springs rising in the hills of the Forest of Dean. The high quality of the brew was due to the 'purity of the water'. By 1870 Thomas Wintle was listed as a maltster, miller, brewer and corn dealer at the Forest Steam Mills in Cinderford, and at the Brewery at Forest House in Mitcheldean, where the buildings still stand.

By 1871 Alfred Wintle at Bill Mills, a married man with two sons looked after by a servant and a nurse, had extended his commitments. He employed a miller and a maltster who lived with their families in separate dwellings at the mill site. The number of people including children living at Bill Mills in 1871 totalled 20 as recorded by the census returns.

Thomas with his other son, Francis, at the Forest Brewery had also expanded the business. A malt house had been added where 'practically all of

This is the last Will and Testament of me
Thomas Bright of Bill Mill in the parish of Weston
under Penyard in the county of Hereford mealman.
I give and devise to my friends William Bennett of
Hownhall in the parish of Weston under Penyard
aforesaid Farmer and Richard Smith of the parish of
Taynton in the county of Gloucester Farmer their heirs
and assigns All my freehold and copyhold messuages
Lands tenements and hereditaments and all other
my real estate of which I shall die seized or possessed
or which I have or shall have power to appoint or be
otherwise entitled to dispose of. To hold the same unto
and to the use of them the said William Bennett
and Richard Smith their heirs and assigns Upon
trust that they or the survivor of them or the heirs or
assigns of such survivor do and shall as soon as
conveniently may be after my decease sell and
absolutely dispose of the same together or in parcels
either by public auction or private sale or by both
those means as to them or him shall seem expedient
with full power to them and him to buy in and to
rescind any contract for sale and to resell without
being responsible for any loss occasioned thereby And
to do and execute all such acts and assurances for
effectuating any such sale as they or he shall think fit.
And I will and declare that the receipt or receipts of
the said William Bennett and Richard Smith or the
survivor of them or the heirs or assigns of such survivor
for the money for which the same hereditaments and

The Will of Thomas Bright 'of Bill Mill' dated 28 January 1865

The Forest Brewery, Mitcheldean (from a colour poster)

the barley used in the brewery was obtained from Herefordshire, one of the best barley districts in the kingdom'. Thomas died in 1888 and Francis took over the brewery which grew to become 'one of the largest individual brewers in the kingdom' and continued until well into the 20th century.

In the 1870s and 1880s all kinds of millstones and miller's tools were available from William Gardner at Gloucester Docks. The company supplied the Wintles' at Bill Mills and in the Forest of Dean with equipment, and in 1870 offered the following:

WM. GARDNER,

Importer of French Burrs, and Manufacturer of Millstones for Grinding all kinds of Grain, Bones, Paint, Cement, Coprolite, Chemicals, &c. Peak and Welsh Millstones direct from the Quarries. Flour Dressing and Smut Machines, Bolters and Bolting Cloths, Machine Wire and Brushes, Cast Steel Mill Pecks, Metal Provers and Staffs, Sack Trucks, and all kinds of Millers' Tools may be had on the shortest notice. Prices of any of the above may be had on application. All orders for exportation and by post promptly attended to.

Lianthony Road, Docks, Gloucester.

Although by 1874 Alfred had established an Engine Yard beside the mill at Bill Mills, it was some years later that steam power was introduced. It appears that milling and malting had declined by 1881 as Alfred was now working himself as a miller and maltster, only employing his wife and two labourers. At this time steampower was being introduced into corn mills so they were no longer reliant upon water. This led to larger modern mills being built on sites with better rail communications, which gradually took over from the smaller waterpowered corn mills.

Alfred obviously had in mind some development plans in 1887, as he acquired a lease from the Trusteds at Parkfield for a 'right to lay down pipes from Flaxridge to Bill Mills'. This was the site of a spring an the slopes of Penyard. But the following year Alfred's life was interrupted by the death of his brother and as an executor he was expected to manage the Forest Brewery at Mitcheldean and the Flour Mill at Cinderford for the trust estate. With these commitments consuming his time from 1888 to 1890, it is unlikely that he paid much attention to the milling and malting at Bill Mills. He must have benefited from his brother's will, because from 1891 a great amount of money was spent on modernising, refurbishing and enlarging Bill Mills to the scale that remains today.

Chapter VI

The Wintles in the 1890s

A Block of building comprising Flour Mills and Aerated Water Manufactory with Store Rooms, Engine and Boiler Houses Stables Sheds Offices together with a Cottage end Garden situate Bill Mills.

Valuation 1895

In 1863 Alfred John Wintle married Ellan Ann, and from 1866 four sons, Tom Clarke, Osman Alfred, Albert John, Wallace Henry, and two daughters were born. Around 1885 Alfred purchased the newly erected Ryefield House on the Gloucester Road in Ross, and shortly afterwards Tom Clarke was living at Elm Cottage In Weston-under-Penyard, where he became involved with parish affairs. At the 1891 census the families of John Bellinger an engineer, Arthur Whitby a mineral water bottler and George Little a miller's loader were living with their families in the three cottages at Bill Mills.

Alfred's expansion and rebuilding of Bill Mills in the 1890s was impressive and showed his talent as a skilled businessman. Before his death in 1895 he installed a roller mill, a grain cleaning department, a beer bottling plant and a mineral water manufactory, all driven by steam and water. His nephew, Francis, the 'Malster, Brewer and Miller' at Mitcheldean and Cinderford had expanded his business and had also purchased between 60 and 70 public houses where his own ales were 'sold exclusively'.

The expansion seems to be reflected in the population of Weston-under-Penyard which, in 1891, had reached a total of 809. There was a village school which had opened in 1865, and a private school run by Kate Riley

Street	*Bild Mills*
Town	*N: Ross*
County	*Herefordshire*
Date	*Dec 21ˢᵗ 92*

To

Messrs. Arth. Guinness, Son & Co., Limited.

GENTLEMEN,

In consideration of your agreeing to supply *us* with your Trade Mark Bottle Label, as per copy annexed hereto, for the purpose of attaching same to the Bottles containing your Porter, *We* hereby agree as follows :—

1. That *we* will attach said Labels only to such Bottles as contain the Porter manufactured by your Company.

2. That *we* will not sell the said Porter in Bottles unless such Bottles bear the said Labels.

3. That *we* will not sell or dispose of any of the said Labels otherwise than by affixing them to Bottles containing Porter obtained from your Company, and bottled by *us*

4. That *we* will not Bottle, nor sell in Bottle, the Porter, Brown Beer, or Stout of any other Brewer, while you continue to supply *us* with your Labels.

5. In case of *our* discontinuing bottling, or should *we* wish to bottle the Porter, Brown Beer, or Stout of any other Brewer, hereby undertake to give due Notice in writing thereof to your Company, and to return any Labels to you that may be in *our* hands.

In case of the contracting party trading under another style, add under Signature "Trading as," etc.

(*Signed*) A. I. W
J. C. W
G A W
} Jⁿ & co
A. Iw & S

Present when Signed by the said } J. Brown

The agreement with Guinness made in 1892 for bottling their product

who later moved to Ross. Most of the population were employed in agriculture on farms where wheat, barley and roots were the main crops grown. In the parish there were three inns, at least two shops, a post office and the services of a blacksmith, wheelwright, joiner, tailor and a builder. Rev. Edward Hawkshaw served as Rector from 1854 to 1912. He lived at the Rectory with his wife Catherine, the daughter of Sir Hungerford Hoskyns from Harewood. Thomas Thompson was the Weslyan minister and Even Watkins served at the Baptist chapel.

The 'high road' between Gloucester and Hereford had been vastly improved by the turnpike trusts before being taken over by the County Council which was formed under the Local Government Act of 1888. The Hereford, Ross and Gloucester Railway opened in 1855 and was worked by the Great Western Railway from 1862. Stations with goods yards were built at Ross and Mitcheldean Road, but the halt at Weston-under-Penyard did not open until 1929. In 1873 the Ross to Monmouth Railway opened with a station at Kerne Bridge and a halt at Walford which was erected at a much later date.

With these improved communications and the funding available to him, it is understandable that Alfred Wintle at Bill Mills took the same advantage as his nephew to expand the business. In 1889 Alfred's storage of 'a stack of fodder containing about twenty tons' was nearby at Parkfields, indicating he lacked sufficient space at Bill Mills. So more space and a modernisation of milling machinery was necessary to deal with growing demands of the 1890s. In this period many brewers borrowed money on a large scale to increase their output, at a time when improved techniques allowed for the bottling of beer.

A Horizontal Compound Tandem Condensing Steam Engine
purchased from Th. Robinson in 1892

Alfred Wintle followed this trend, but coupled it with with the manufacturing of mineral water to satisfy the more temperate drinker.

The Flaxridge spring on the slopes on Penyard Hill marked the Ross parish boundary In 1709 it had been visited by John Kyrle who 'dipped a wooden can in the well, and drank from the spring'. In 1886 Alfred laid a line of water pipes from the spring to Bill Mills under the terms of a lease from Parkfields. The water was then carbonized and bottled at Bill Mills and sold as Aerated Mineral Water. In 1892 he purchased another aerated water business from Richard Williams and Sons in the Forest of Dean. This purchase included the goodwill of the company, the plant, bottles, jars, cases, tanks, ingredients, a van, a wagon, a gray horse, harness, bridles and a desk with cupboards and drawers.

By 1891 machinery had been installed at Bill Mills to bottle, label and cork beer which came from Guinness's at Bristol, along with Bass, Ratcliff and Gretton at Burton-on-Trent and Allsopp's also from Burton. Large quantities

A. J. WINTLE & SONS,

MILLERS

AND

Mineral Water Manufacturers,

BOTTLERS OF

ALLSOPP'S ALES

AND

GUINNESS'S DUBLIN STOUT.

N.B.—A. J. W. & S. have just put in a complete Roller Mill, with all latest improvements, on Messrs. Robinson's System, at

BILL MILLS, nr. ROSS.

H. & S.

An advert placed in an 1891 trade directory

Bill Mills circa *1880*

of beer in casks were delivered by rail to Mitcheldean Road Station, or occasionally to Ross Station, then transported by horse drawn wagons to Bill Mills. After bottling the beer, the empty casks ware returned, and the bottled beer, carefully labelled, was placed in wooden cases before being distributed. Amongst the records is an unusual recipe for 'Brewing Bassara Ale' made from a tin of extract mixed with cane sugar, water and yeast. It is doubtful whether this was ever brewed at Bill Mills.

It was not until the invention of steampower that the waterwheel had a serious rival. Steam engines provided more power but were expensive and needed a constant supply of fuel. Unlike the waterwheel, which could be started and used within seconds, the steam engine took several hours before 'getting up a head of steam'. Although steampower had already been introduced at Bill Mills, it was in 1891 that a new steam engine and boiler were purchased from Thomas Robinson and delivered to 'the nearest railway station'. The improvements and modernisation of Bill Mills were carried out by Robinsons, milling engineers from Rochdale, William Gardner, a millwright and manufacturer of millstones from Gloucester, and W.H. Smith, the local builder and contractor at Weston-under-Penyard.

The mineral water factory, circa *1900s*

A cockle and barley cylinder

From the plans and correspondence with these companies it appears that a former malt house was raised by nine foot to house the four-storied flour mill. A wall was taken out near the waterwheel, the building made good where it connected with the malt kiln and provision was made to house the new boiler and engine. Thirteen iron-framed windows were inserted in the flour mill, similar to those already installed in the factory. The floors and roof of the old corn mill were repaired, the store house and cottages were whitewashed, a furnace was moved to a 'new position in the cottage', and all the guttering and drainage was made good.

As Alfred was no longer living at the mill site, it appears that Bill Mill House was converted to a store. The expansion of Bill Mills continued throughout 1892 and 1893 after Alfred had acquired additional land from John Tertius Southall at Parkfields. Further plans were made by Robinsons to increase the plant in the flour mill, and to make provision for the cockle and barley cylinders as shown in the illustrations. Other work carried out at this time included repairing the coach house, underpinning the cellar wall, fixing the pig cot and installing the clock, which still survives as a prominent feature on the flour mill.

With the latest machinery at Bill Mills and Alfred's skills as a miller, it is not surprising to learn that in 1892 he won a silver medal for the 'Best Sample

Smart merchandising was the best way of reflecting the quality of Wintles' products

of Flour' at the Milling and Bakery Exhibition held at the Agricultural Hall in London. His entry in Class IV, that included details of the processing involved, read:

> Wintle, A.J. & Sons, Bill Mills, Ross, Herefordshire. Milled, June 8; system, T. Robinson & Son's; cleaning machinery used, Aspirator, Eureka, Smutter, and Brush machine; purifier used, 'Koh-i-nor'.

The business interests of the Wintles at Bill Mills and at the Forest Brewery, Mitcheldean, may be followed through a collection of ledgers, receipt books, dispatch notes, invoices, letters and other documentation which have been deposited at the Hereford Record Office. Although fragmentary they do provide a fairly comprehensive picture of rural businesses during the 1890s. Although in similar trades it appears that the two relatives worked independently of one another, although there there was some small exchange of milling products, and some ale brewed at the Forest Brewery was bottled at Bill Mills.

Steam engine in the factory with its guards, circa *1890s*

This collection includes a bound book recording an inventory of household furniture, stock in trade, horses and waggons, farming stock and other effects of 'the late Thomas Wintle Esq.,' in 1888. There is also a bundle of invoices for iron and hardware purchased in Ross and Gloucester, receipts for waggon and carriage repairs carried out by T.W. Bailey at Ross, and orders for flour, stout and mineral water from as far afield as Glasgow, Manchester and Liverpool.

The *Ross Gazette* of 21 November 1895 reported the death of A.J. Wintle at the age of 57 at Ryefield House in Ross after a five months' illness. The 'Malster and

Miller' at Bill Mills 'was well known and highly esteemed by a large circle of friends'. The funeral cortège left Ryefield House conveying the coffin made by his builder from Weston-under-Penyard. Three carriages conveyed his family and relatives, and a 'toll was rang from the belfry of Ross parish church' as they left the town. He was 'interned' in the family vault at Oxenhall, where a 'muffled bell was peeled'.

In his will Alfred had appointed his four sons—Tom Clark, Osman Alfred, Albert John and Wallace Henry as trustees. To his wife, Ellen Ann, he left his 'plate, linen, china, glass, books, pictures, prints, wines, liquors, furnishings other household effects and my carriages and horses'. She also benefited from an annuity and the 'residence and premises known as Ryefield House'. After his death this was valued at £1,000, and the rest of his 'Real Estate' which included three cottages, flour mills, aerated water manufactory, stores, engine and boiler houses, sheds, offices and six acres of land at Bill Mills were worth £1,822 10s. Ryefield House was sold, but Bill Mills remained in the family.

Chapter VII

The Final Years

Bill Mills has always appealed to me as an a strange, unique, little group of buildings on a quiet little country road from Pontshill through to Coughton. It takes two violent right angle turns and between these two right angle turns are a substantial group of buildings, obviously used for commercial purposes with some smaller residences, obviously cottages of an early age on the other side of the road. The engineering works of the mill race, sluice and weir seem to come up out of nowhere in the middle of rather beautiful countryside.

Derek Preece, unpublished mss., 1977

After the death of Alfred John Wintle in 1895, the milling, malting, bottling and mineral water manufacturing was continued at Bill Mills by his sons Tom Clark and Osman Alfred. In 1896 the stock of the mill included flour, bran, meal, maize, barley, beans, and wheat. In the factory were large quantities of ale, stout, minerals, sugar, essence, corks, bottles and cases of beer. Order forms of 1897 show that soda, lemonade, gingerade, ginger beer, orange champagne, cordials and mineral water were manufactured in the factory, and that ale and stout were bottled on the premises.

Further modernisation took place in 1899 when foundations were laid for a 'Tangye Horizontal Engine', installed to either replace or assist the existing Robinson steam engine. As the mill was increasing its productivity, maybe two engines together with waterpower were required. The Tangye engine and boiler have since been restored and at present are housed in the lower floor of the former flour mill.

Wintle's beer waggon, circa *1900s*

Wintle's steam lorry, circa *1900s*

In 1903 Tom Clark was 37 years old when he made a 'Statutory Declaration' that Bill Mills comprised of 'a Steam Flour Mill, a Corn Grist Mill, Counting House, Aerated water Manufactory, Store Houses, and small Yard adjoining a Stream of Water with Mill Ponds, Two Cottages, Stables, Engine Shed, Cart Shed and Garden'. This declaration was made so that Tom and Osman could apply for a mortgage to purchase 'two undivided fourth parts' from their brothers Albert John and Wallace Henry. Albert was living at Cedar Villa in Ross, and Wallace was working as the brewery manager for his cousin Francis Wintle at Mitcheldean, where 'mild and bitter ales and stout' were brewed and 'sent out in casks'. Francis supplied ale to his numerous public-houses and to many private families who enjoyed the 'beverage' known for its 'purity and wholesomeness not excelled anywhere'. In addition to his brewing interests Francis still operated the flour mill at Cinderford which was equipped with the latest machinery.

With the business arrangements at Bill Mills settled by 1905, Tom remained living at Elm Cottage and Osman at Edenhurst in Ross. Apart from the milling, bottling and mineral water production the brothers had become retail and wholesale agents for 'Bass's Ales, Guinness's Dublin Stout, and for Forest Brewery, Mitcheldean supplied in casks or bottles'. Steam lorries and horse-drawn vehicles were used to deliver their goods. Horses often needed to be replaced and a letter from a supplier from the Bollin in Walford reads 'If you are in want of cheap useful horses for your pop wagons there are two to be sold here without reserve that would do the job well'.

By 1914 Osman had moved to Penyard Lodge within walking distance of the mill where the business, still called Alfred John Wintle and Sons, was also bottling 'lager', apparently an early date for its consumption in this country. During the dark days of the First World War the flour mill ceased, the machinery was scrapped, and 'all that was left was a bit of coarse grinding for the farmers to feed their stock'. From this time the water from the Castle Brook was used chiefly for mineral water manufacture together with the spring water from the Flaxridge.

After the death of J.T. Southall, his estate, Parkfields was put up for auction in 1917. The 'Special Conditions' of the sale included 'a line of Water Pipes from the Flaxridge to Bill Mill crossing Nos. 400, 401, 402 and 453, the right to lay these Pipes having been leased by the Vendors' Testator to Mr. A.J. Wintle for a period of 42 years from 1886, at the yearly rent of £29 under a lease which will be produced at the time of the Sale. The tenant is under

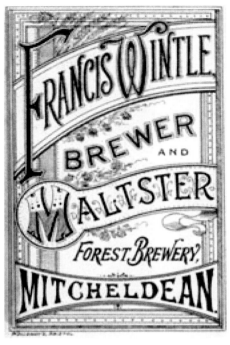

Above: Front cover and price list of an advertising handout of circa *1910*
Below: An advert in a trade directory of 1905

liability to keep the pipes in repair'. The numbers represent the fields named Well Field, Baker's Orchard, Baker's Meadow and Old Orchard on the Tithe Map of 1838.

After the First World War a young man, Charlie Cole was employed by A.J. Wintle and Sons, 'down at the Mill at the factory there'. Others employed there included the foreman, Arthur Wiggin, and Harry Roberts described as the head boy. They worked a 12 hour day from 6 a.m. to 6 p.m. with two breaks for breakfast and dinner. Charlie found the work 'terrible boring' at a place where no girls were employed and where the boys wasted bottles of pop by squirting it over one another. After a short period at Bill Mills Charlie moved onto another job at Hopes Ash Farm before returning at a later period.

By 1921 Tom and Osman's mortgage was reconveyed due to the death of the mortgagee. The following year their cousin Francis at the Forest Brewery in Mitcheldean was suffering from ill-health and decided to retire from business, which 'he had most successfully carried on, and his father before him, for nearly Sixty Years'. In 1923 'The Forest Steam Brewery together with 72 Freehold Licensed Properties, also Cottages, Shops, Land, Etc.' were for sale. The business, it was suggested, offered to 'Brewers an excellent opportunity of acquiring one of the best known concerns in the West. The Brewery and Maltings are up to date, and the Beer has an unrivalled reputation for many miles around'.

The licensed properties included the Weston Cross Inn at Weston-under-Penyard, the Railway Hotel at Lea and several pubs in Ross and the Forest of Dean. A memo dated 1923 indicates that an offer was made to Francis, but he 'seemed a bit concerned about the purchaser keeping the brewing going. He thought It such a pity to close it down'. Later that year the Forest Brewery was sold and the new purchaser registered the business as a limited liability company named 'Wintle's Brewery Ltd.', which by 1937 was in the hands of the Cheltenham Original Brewery Company Ltd., who did indeed close it down.

During the 1920s Bill Mills was operating as a corn and flour merchants, beer agents and a mineral water manufactory run by Tom and Osman until 1927 when Osman died. William Norman, one of his four sons, then moved to Bill Mills to take the place of his father. He lived in the upper floor of the warehouse which had been converted into a flat. He had married Clara Doris, and their children including Joan and Doreen, who can recall the creaking of the waterwheel, the rumbling of the floor boards, and the sound of machinery

An advert in the 1936 Ross Guide

48

A delivery lorry in circa *1920*

filling their ears. They remember with fondness the bustling life of the mill and exploring the surrounding countryside during their school holidays.

In the 1930s the mill was only manufacturing mineral water and bottling Bass, Worthington, Guinness, Stout, Marston's Ales and Whiteway's Cyder. These operations continued into the 1940s with the waterwheel and engine powering the machinery until electricity and mains water was laid through the Castle Brook valley. Charlie Cole was back 'repairing all the wooden pop bottle cases down at Bill Mills' and 'the sluice gates on the pond and the spokes on the water wheel'. These jobs were attended to on a Saturday afternoon when the mill had stopped working for the weekend. Apparently the wheel became more rickety, eventually broke and was replaced by a six horsepower diesel engine.

In 1958, at the age of 60, Norman, known as Norry, took on Brian Jenkins to manage A.J. Wintle and Sons. Brian moved to Ross with his father, L.C. Jenkins, a cork merchant, who continued this business at Bill Mills for a short time. Brian became a shareholder in the Wintle business and eventually

Bill Mills in circa *1900*

purchased the company at a time when it was concerned with bottling soft drinks under the Wintle brand, and beer in returnable glass bottles. 'Brian's plan was to build the company to be a significant local manufacturer and distributor to the licensed and leisure trade. The company sold many factored goods such as Bulmers Cider, Babycham, Britvic, Schweppes and bottled bears. He also tried wines and spirits with moderate success', says Brian's son Ian.

Brian increased sales by introducing draught soft drinks in the late 1960s, which became the main profit maker for the company. In 1975 a valuation of the Bill Mills property was made by Tony Netting for business purposes, and in 1977 the buildings at Bill Mills were listed as grade II for their historical and architectural importance. Both these reports provide a detailed account of the buildings when they were still in use as a soft drinks factory, employing about 20 local people and providing 300,000 gallons of different soft drinks a year. This was part of a plan to market drinks by working with three other independent family businesses in the country, and shows the dramatic increase once water for soft drinks became available from the mill's own borehole sunk in 1962.

Around 1979 the company changed its name to Dayla Soft Drinks Western Limited. In 1980 Brian's son Ian joined the business and eventually took over as managing director. This allowed Brian time to research the history of the mill and preserve the buildings. He converted the outbuildings into holiday cottages, restored the mill and reinstated the waterwheel. In 1989 a modern factory was built at Bill Mills to house Dayla, and although a short and limited use was made of the old mill buildings it was obvious that a new use was needed to ensure their survival.

Having changed the name of the company again in 1998 to Dayla Liquid Packing Limited, business in the new factory continued to thrive and grow. The main offices were still housed in the mill buildings, in fact in the old flat where Norry Wintle had lived in the 1920s. Around 1995 Ian Jenkins made several attempts to reinstate the mill and to give the buildings a useful commercial purpose. Ideas were developed to create various uses, including a paper museum, a group of offices, even a hotel, but none were deemed viable.

By the end of the Millennium business had grown to such an extent that it was decided to move all Dayla's manufacturing from Bill Mills to a new site purchased at Ross-on-Wye. After at least 650 years of uninterrupted industrial use plans were put in place to convert the mill at Bill Mills to private houses. Great care was taken to preserve the historical integrity of the buildings; the mill wheel was again returned to working condition and the industrial and architectural features were protected as far as possible.

The end of an era? Well certainly a change and a break from the past. How fortunate those people now who view Bill Mills in its new life. Probably few of them are aware of the wonderful history that this secret corner of the world holds. Whilst it is unlikely that industry will ever return to the Castle Brook, the mill at Bill Mills has more than played its part in providing iron and flour, paper and grain, and beer and soft drinks to the people of Herefordshire and beyond.

Sources

CHAPTER I
Bonnor, Thomas *Ten Picturesque Views*, 1798
Cave, Brian *Weston & Lea*, 1982
Coates, Stan & D. Tucker *Water Mills of the Middle Wye Valley*, 1985
Dreghorn, William *Geology in the Forest of Dean*, 1968
Fosbroke, T.D. *Ariconensia*, 1821
Hurley, Heather *The Old Roads of South Herefordshire*, 1992

The Railway Magazine, 1909
Woolhope Club Transactions, 1903, 1959

Hereford Record Office
Estate Survey (Eccleswall), 1699
Cobrey Estate Plan, 1822
Weston-under-Penyard Tithe Map, 1838
Agreement, 1840
E. Cassey, Herefordshire Map, 1858

Gloucester Record Office
Thomas Telford Mail Coach Route, 1824

Public Record Office
Calendar of Patent Rolls, 1549

CHAPTER II
Coplestone-Crow, Bruce *Herefordshire Place Names*, 1989
Duncumb., J. *Continuation of the History of Herefordshire*, Vol. III
Hart, Cyril *The Industrial History of Dean*, 1971
Major, J.K., *Watermills and Windmills*, 1986
Nicholls, H.G. *Iron Making in the Forest of Dean*, 1866
Robinson, C. *Manors and Mansions of Herefordshire*, 1872
Schubert, H.R. *History of the British Iron and Steel industry*, 1957
Smith, A.H. *English Place Names*, 1970

B.G.A.S. Vol. 6, 1991
Industries of Herefordshire in Bygone Times, Newcolmes Society, 1937
Woolhope Club Transactions, 1903, 1919, 1928, 1936
G.S.I.A., 1974

Hereford Record Office
Walwyn Records
Hope Mansell Lease, 1362
Hope Mansell Terrier, 1589, 1607
Weston-under-Penyard Terrier, 1623
Weston-under-Penyard Parish Registers
Entries of Lloyds in Weston-under-Penyard Registers
Plan of Billmill Paper Mill, *c.*1820

Gloucester Record Office
Colchester Papers
Inq PM 1638, printed 1893, pt 2

CHAPTERS III & IV
Cobbett, William *Rural Rides*, 1821
Coleman, D.C. *The British Paper Industry 1495-1860*, 1958
Hart, Cyril *The Industrial History of Dean*, 1971
Heath, Charles *Excursion Down the Wye*, 1828
Mills, S. & P. Riemer *The Mills of Gloucestershire*, 1984
Shorter, A.H. *Paper Making in England*, 1957

The Complete Peerage, Vol. III, 1913
Hereford Journal, 1774
G.S.A.I., 1974
Wind and Water Mills, 1981, 1985
B.G.A.S., 1952
DNB, 1917 ed
Woolhope Club Transactions 1949, 1975

Talbot Papers, Ms708-1606, Lambeth Palace Library
Robin Clark Mss, Birmingham Central Library Archives
Lease for Perry Barr, 1642, Birmingham Central Library Archives
H.E. Simmons Papers, National Science Museum, nd
Isaac Taylor's Map of Herefordshire, 1754, 1786
Department of Environment Report, 1977

Sun Fire Insurance, 1782 Guildhall Library
Brian Jenkins' notes, c.1980
Derek Preece's notes on Bill Mill, 1977
Mortimer Cross Guide, 1997
Charlecote Mill Guide, nd

Hereford Record Office
Bill Mill records
Deed of Trust for the benefit of Lord Coleraine's creditors, 1773
Weston-under-Penyard Parish registers
Weston-under-Penyard Land Tax Returns

Gloucester Record Office
Joseph Lloyd Inventory, 1803
Viney family records

CHAPTER V
Evans, G.E. *The farm and the Village*, 1969
Hopkins, R.T. *Old watermills and Windmills*, c.1933
Raistrick, Arthur *Industrial Archaeology*, 1972

City of Hereford Arch. Com. Gunns Mills, Jan. 1988
Industrial Gloucestershire, 1904

Paper Excise Letters, 1816, 1832, Birmingham Central Library Archives

Hereford Record Office
Weston-under-Penyard Census 1841-1881
Herefordshire Directories 1851, 1867
Bill Mill Records
Thomas Wintle Trust Estate

CHAPTER VI
Coates, Stan & D. Tucker *Water Mills of the Middle Wye*, 1983
Fosbroke, T.D. *The Wye Tour*, 1833
Lovett, M. *Brewing and Breweries*, 1996
Raistrick, Arthur *Industrial Archaeology*, 1972
Richardson, L. *Wells and Springs of Herefordshire*, 1935
Richmond, L. & A. Turton, *The Brewing Industry*, 1990
Smith, William *Herefordshire Railways*, 1998

Herefordshire Directory, 1891
Industrial Gloucestershire, 1904
Ross Gazette, 1895

Hereford Record Office
Thomas Wintle Trust Estate
Bill Mills records
Parkfields Sale Particulars, 1917

CHAPTER VII
Cole, Charlie *My Life at Dancing Green*, 1997
Richmond, L. & A. Turton *The Brewing Industry*, 1990

Herefordshire Directory 1902, 1905
Ross Advertizer, 1977
Ross Gazette, 1983, 1987

Hereford Record Office
Bill Mill Records
Thomas Wintle Trust Estate
Wintle's Additional deposit

Gloucester Record Office
The Forest Steam Brewery Sale Particulars, 1923